GUITAR TAB NOTEBOOK

6 String Guitar tab paper on 100 pages + 10 extra pages with chords and lots of infos

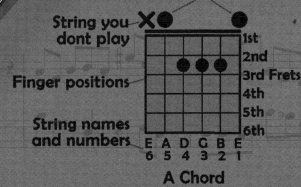
A Chord

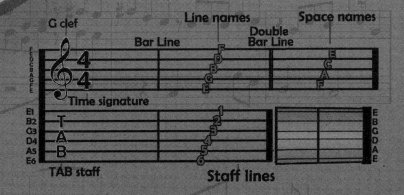

Head

String Post

Tuning Pegs

Neck

Nut

E A D G B E

Fretboard

1
2
3
4
5
6
7
8
9
10
11
12

Frets

Body

Reading a Chord Box

Open strings you play

String you dont play ✗

Finger positions

1st
2nd
3rd Frets
4th
5th
6th

String names and numbers

E A D G B E
6 5 4 3 2 1

A Chord

G clef

Line names

Bar Line

Double Bar Line

Space names

E D C B A G F E

$\frac{4}{4}$

F
D
B
G
E

E
C
A
F

Time signature

E1
B2
G3
D4
A5
E6

T
A
B

1
2
3
4
5
6

TAB staff

Staff lines

E
B
G
D
A
E

Notes that make up a chord

Major

Chord	1	3	5
A Chord	A	C#	E
B Chord	B	D#	F#
C Chord	C	E	G
D Chord	D	F#	A
E Chord	E	G#	B
F Chord	F	A	C
G Chord	G	B	D

Minor

Chord	1	3	5
A Chord	A	C	E
B Chord	B	D	F#
C Chord	C	Eb	G
D Chord	D	F	A
E Chord	E	G	B
F Chord	F	G#	C
G Chord	G	A#	D

Chord for the major keys

Keys	Chords		
	I	IV	V
Key of A	A	D	E
Key of B	B	E	F
Key of C	C	F	G
Key of D	D	G	A
Key of E	E	A	B
Key of F	F	B	C
Key of G	G	C	D

Arpeggios

1	3	5	7
A	C#	E	G#
B	D#	F#	A#
C	E	G	B
D	F#	A	C#
E	G#	B	D#
F	A	C	E
G	B	D	F#

Frets (E A D G B E)

Fret	E	A	D	G	B	E
1.	F	A#	D#	G#	C	F
2.	F#	B	E	A	C#	F#
3.	G	C	F	A#	D	G
4.	G#	C#	F#	B	D#	G#
5.	A	D	G	C	E	A
6.	A#	D#	G#	C#	F	A#
7.	B	E	A	D	F#	B
8.	C	F	A#	D#	G	C
9.	C#	F#	B	E	G#	C#
10.	D	G	C	F	A	D
11.	D#	G#	C#	F#	A#	D#
12.	E	A	D	G	B	E

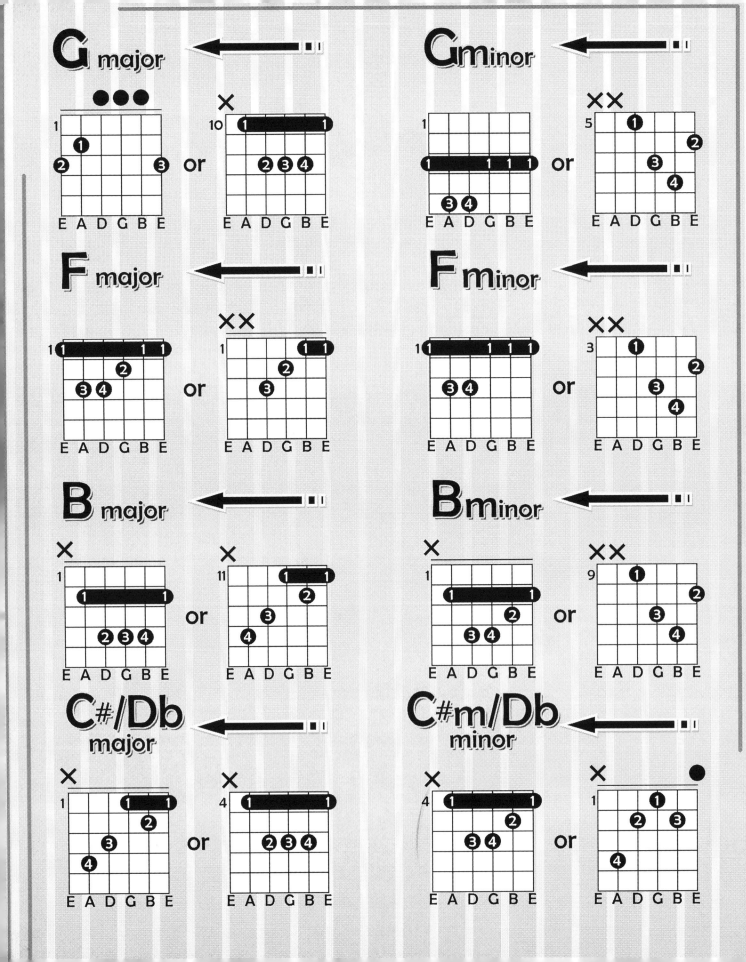

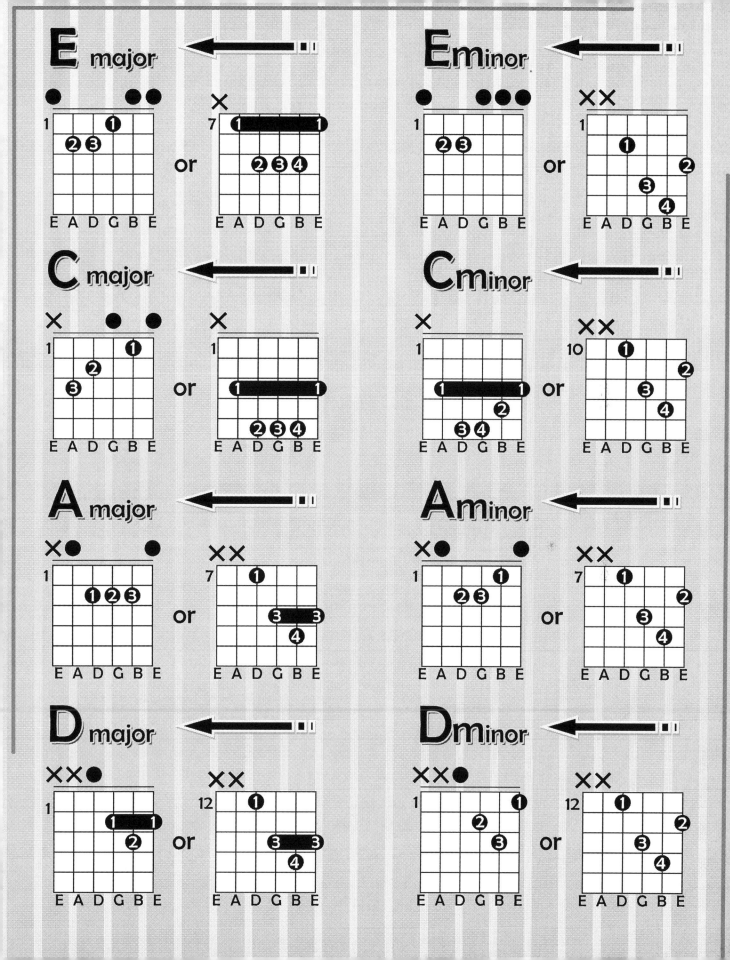

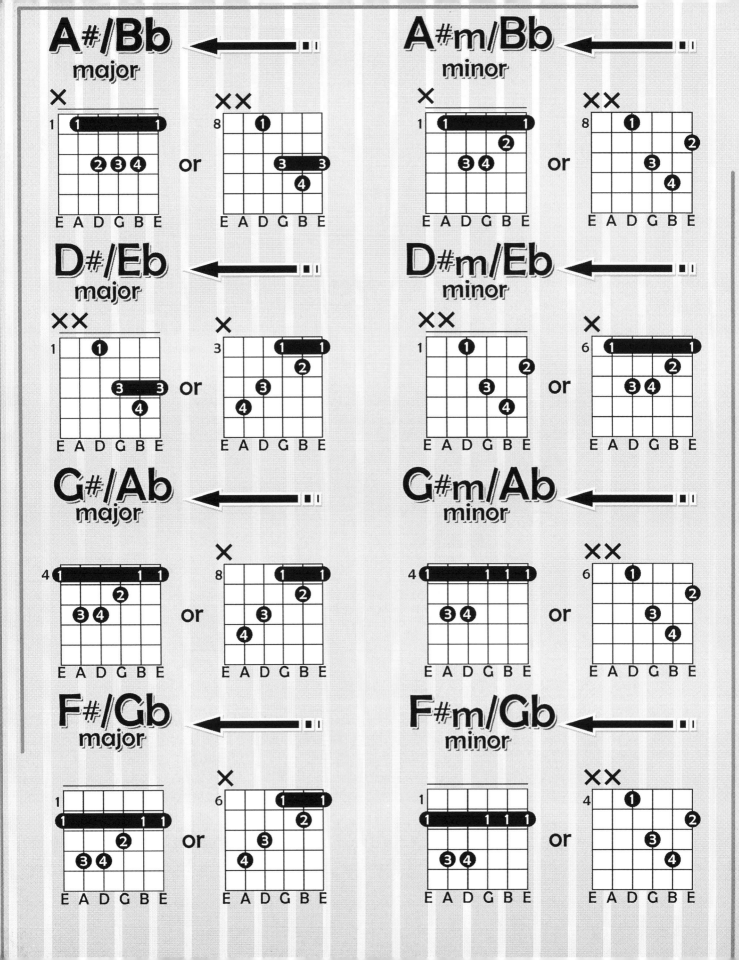

How to read Guitar Tablature

The Basic Layout

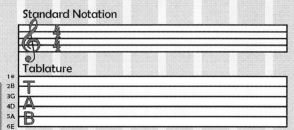

A Tab (or tablature) has a standard notation on top and a tab on the bottom. Guitars usually have six strings, and the first thing you will have to learn is the name of all the strings. The top string represents the thickest string, and it is called the 6th string or highE string. The next string is called 5th string or A string for similar reasons. The other string in order are 4th or D string, 3rd or G string, 2nd or B string and 1st or e-string (thinnest string). As the 1st and 6th string are both E notes, we distinguish the 1st string by writing it in a smaller case "e". Is important to remember that Tabs usually have six horizontal lines, which represents the six strings of the guitar and you will always read them from left to right (You will only play multiple notes at the same time when they are stacked on top of one another).

Notes and Chords

The numbers in a tablature represents the frets where you will put your fingers on. Notes: Single numbers from left to right represent a melody line or solo. Chords: Vertically stacked numbers represent a chord.

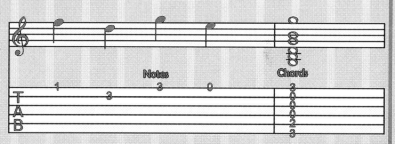

Palm Muting & Muted Notes

These are the more common elements that you will see when learning to play your favorite songs. Palm Muting: Is represented by a "P.M." marker. The little dashes represent how long you should continue to palm mute the notes. Muted Notes: Dead notes, or muted notes, are represented by an "X" on a particular string. When you see a dead note you should mute the note with either your left or right hand and play that note so the pitch is completely muted.

Bending

Bending is a common element of Tab. You can know when to bend a note by an upward pointing arrow next to one or more numbers. The distance you are to bend the note will be defined by an indicator next to the arrow. This could be a "full" or a "1/2" bend, or in other words, a full bend means bending up a whole step and a half bend means bending up a half step.

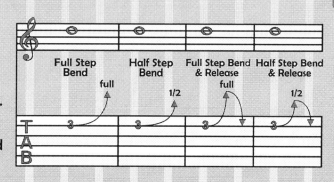

Sliding

Sliding is represented by a fret number, a line, and then another fret number. The line will be slanted up or down depending on if you are sliding from a higher pitch to a lower pitch or vice versa.

Hammer-ons & Pull-offs

You can identify hammer-ons and pull-offs by a little slur or arc between two or more adjacent notes. They are also frequently referred to as "Legato".

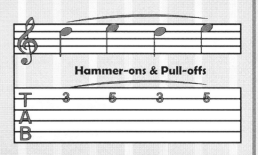

Vibratio

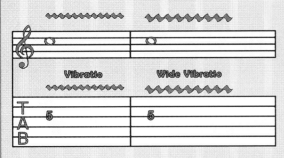

Vibrato is when you repeatedly bend and release a note over and over for an expressive vocal effect. This is usually represented by a squiggly line over a note. You can identify how intense or wide the vibrato should be by the thickness or boldness of the squiggly line.

Downstrokes & Upstrokesa

Downstroke indicators look like a squared off upside down "U", and upstrokes indicators look like a downward facing arrow. If the composer wrote a piece of music

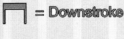

with a specific picking pattern you will see picking indicators, and If they didn't you will not see any indicators, therefore you can experiment with your own picking patterns.

Note	English	American	Rest
	Long	Quadruple whole note	
	Breve	Double whole note	
	Semibreve	Whole note	
	Minim	Half note	
	Crotchet	Quarter note	
	Quaver	Eighth note	
	Semiquaver	Sixteenth note	
	Demisemiquaver	Thirty-second note	

Key Signature	Added #	Major Key	Minor Key	Key Signature	Added ♭	Major Key	Minor Key
	F#	G major	E minor		B♭	F major	D minor
	C#	D major	B minor		E♭	B♭ major	G minor
	G#	A major	F# minor		A♭	E♭ major	C minor
	D#	E major	C# minor		D♭	A♭ major	F minor
	A#	B major	G# minor		G♭	D♭ major	B♭ minor
	E#	F# major	D# minor		C♭	G♭ major	E♭ minor
	B#	C# major	A# minor		F♭	C♭ major	A♭ minor

We hope you have enjoyed our Guitar Music Manuscript book as much as we enjoyed working on it. If so, please leave a review in our book's page on the Amazon website. This helps us to make even better books for you. Thank you for your support and learning music with us!

www.bookcreators.net
www.twitter.com/bookcreators
www.facebook.com/bookcreators
www.instagram.com/welovemakingbooks

Printed in Great Britain
by Amazon